THE 14 KEYS

POWER, SUCCESS, AND TRANSFORMATION

UNLOCKED

CHIEF YUYA

ANU NATION
GLOBAL

ISBN-13: 978-0-9980966-0-5

The 14 Keys
HRU Yuya T. Assaan-ANU
ANU Publishing
www.AlphaOmegaStore.com

HRU Yuya T. Assaan-ANU
"The 14 Keys"
ISBN-13: 978-0-9980966-0-5

© 2016, HRU Yuya T. Assaan-ANU
ANU Nation
www.ANUNation.org

LIVICATION

I bestow the impact of this tome to Baba Robert Lee and Iya
Gertrude Lee.
To each, and every, Elder who took the time to share their wisdom with me, this book is the testimony of your brilliance.
To all the humble students of Sadulu House and the ANU Nation
family, I thank you for your support and fervent commitment to
this sacred endeavor.
To all of my light bearers, you are the lustrous reflection of all I
dream. Ngiyabonga.
To my children, born and unborn, all this is for you. Your Baba
is clearing the road for you to be the greatest champions of the
resurrection of our ancestors. Ngiyakuthanda nonke!

CONTENTS

INTRODUCTION

CHIEF YUYA

THE 14 KEYS

14 Afrakan Principles

The outlining concept of the 14 Keys was presented to me by one of my beloved family Elders, Abishai Ben Reuben-Bey, one night as we discussed some of the issues that were plaguing the small town we claimed as home. Baba Abishai and I had spent many years discussing and plotting ways to awaken OUR people to a healthier state of being. The conversation, on this night, was not unlike countless ones had before with the exception of a glint of wisdom he imparted that grew, with time and examination, into a lustrous gem.

One cold December night while giving Baba Abishai a ride to a local Kwanzaa event he was facilitating we spoke about the need for a Maat'ic balancing and mass healing for our people. Baba Abishai said, "we have all the principles we need between the Nguzo Saba and the Principles of Maat". He referred to them as the "14 Afrakan principles". It was a glorious spark of wisdom handed to me by this beloved child of Sango. He said nothing more of it but, I told him I would build further on it. That was over ten years before the release of this work.

That conversation, had so many years ago, never strayed far from my foremost thoughts. I knew I needed to put the theory into practise. Baba Abishai and I watered a seed implanted in the spirit of our fellowship by our Ancestors.

Consider a rudimentary collection of concepts that could be memorized quickly and applied to numerous situations, we were facing. Despite the simplicity of such a conception, as with any primal concept or symbol, the "rabbit hole" runs deep. Reverently examining these massive ideas and creating a contemporary interpretation was a daunting task.

This work strives to RE-present the amazing fruits of the abysmal pool of Afrakan wisdom to the world so that we can heal the individual and community. We will use the terms "14 Afrakan Principles" and "14 keys" interchangeably Admittedly, I use the word "key" as opposed to "principle" because of the vision conceived by the word. When many think of a "key", they consider something that unlocks a puzzle or entryway to another reality. In truth, a key is a principle. To usher in a new era, new principles must be adopted and old ones adapted. This book revises Afrakan principles and unwraps the value of their universal employment.

CHIEF YUYA

THE CHALLENGE

CHIEF YUYA

THE 14 KEYS

We are existence enshrouded within a sheathing of expiring flesh experiencing a distancing from our divine credos and durable congruity with the eminent mind. This is the honorarium for our maturation into humankind. Through this life discipline there is a lengthening of our breadth of knowledge by way of information obtainment and conversely, more often than not, a compaction of the spiritual form. This mental ripening is considered to be the burgeoning of the human ego. It is through this partisan human ego that we discover the unique tone and call of our own purpose for life. Conversely, this call pulls us away from our sentience of belonging to a greater gnosis and spirit body. Intellectual and celestial excursion through the annals of self inquest, commonly, result in a cultural amnesia followed by a never-ending chase for "truth".

The personal consideration of the divine mind offers a miraculous disclosure of the "self". Additionally, the presence of an aggregate body of individuals on one accord is the requisite for the efficacy and serviceability of a community. These aggregate bodies/communities create norms and systems that allow for a functional state within the world-wide context. It is through many moments of ritual and deliberation that communal traditions are conceived. When these community members come together and reflect on their story and the affect they have had in the world, they make determinations that evolve those traditions to maintain their presence and upwardly mobile developmental heading.

This evolution is a movement of the whole self by way of spiraling towards a higher, or even, mythological state of presence. If we can see organic evolution as the wind, then let us envision the key principles of culture as the earth element. Nominally the word "culture" attaches us to the mechanism of cultivation and agriculture, which highlight our obligations to the earth. The earth is the shared ground of transmutation for all corporeal occupancies. One must trod upon its firm but, receptive, surface to feel the transforming task of living. The cultivation of principles and mores that ease this transformation and garner stability copulate with the ever coursing spirit/wind of evolution much like our Kemetic "Geb and Nut" giving birth to ASR, AST, SET, and NBT HT.

In order for this evolution to occur there must be a steadfast platform of tried and true and proven norms (earth). Stability breeds stability.

Linking to the harmonious saneness of our ancient, and adaptive, sentience stipulates that we tap into our primal instincts. These primal instincts simplify our being-ness without incessant beguilement from the egotistical cerebration. So, the principles that we build and evolve our creation on top of should reflect our own primal traits and inborn significance. For example, there are what we would call "universal languages" that exist throughout the planet. Music, dance, spiritual ritual, love, lust, and other elemental forces can transcend the bounds of fabricated language and prejudgment. Anytime we do something that is primal in root we can bond to our deeper wisdom and awareness of holism.

In community erecting endeavors these foundations of wisdom must be agreed upon in order to build the structures and institutions that sustain this and the future generation. As individuals categorically do not agree on every single point held within a society, it is the primal value that must be extracted, when needed, in order to continue the enlargement of a group. These primal values even serve to resolve disagreement and expose the compunction of disputes as being endemic to an older issue or an extraneous one introduced by beings outside the community.

Today, many lack an easily referenced set of norms for community rearing aims. We find ourselves debating dogmatic ideas that have nothing to do with the production of a firm and secure foundation where unified culture can meet. Sometimes this is a result of coming into what we hastily label as "consciousness". The itineraries of approach are so diversified, that it is very easy to make the path the speculative achievement and forget the reason or original arrival point that we were initially targeting. For instance, if a group of separate individuals made the decision to invest in varied indigenous spiritual systems, respectively, in order to connect to one primal pulse, it would stand to reason that eventually each individual would end in the same mental/spiritual space. That field referenced would be the space of primal vibration. However, if one were to lose sight of the originating intent, then each indigenous system now becomes a destination of distraction. In this example there is no coefficient cohesiveness, only estrangement despite the fact that all set out on the same mission.

Far too many fall under the delusion that this generation of the "consciously aware" is the first of its kind. Terms like "New Age" do not help to dispel the myth of a "new thing occurring under the sun". However, everything that is beholden evolves. It is the nature of energy. In order for any force to come into the perceptual attentiveness of another being it must be energized. If it has fervor, it has spirited. Spirit is the evolving spiral of evolution. So, in effect, we are not creating beginning norms but, we are spiriting the old ones, thus evolving them into re-birthed creeds and keys. This is no different from our spiritual mythology which describes narratives of different archetypes replacing each other in their respective roles (for example – ANPU to ASR). We feed our old ways in order for them to emerge in current times and be enhanced. All things must evolve. If we do not nourish the old, we never realize the newer. This is similar to the process of feeding your ancestors to bring forth newer children. Those newer children are your next evolutionary stage but, they are also ancestors who have returned.

Without ritual there is no community. Community is prolonged on the evolving principles and keys to primal cognizance.

Without ritual there is NO community.

It is the ritual that binds individuals together and feeds those past standards so, that they can become the new way. Culture always seeks to grow and find a place in a fluctuating world environment.

Based on the importance of communal ceremony we can say organization should not be the priority but, rather collusive transmittable imperatives should be. These compulsions and norms should be ritualized, socially, so the organization is formed from the ingenious expansion of those primal norms. You will have your society of magi, your society or farmers, society of drummers, society of garment makers, society of nobility, and so forth all within the walls of your familial coalition. Through group ritual and transmission of celestial designation, characters are marked in a group setting. Individual roles are identified for the furtherance of the collective.

Once this commonwealth is formed it then becomes a self regenerative organism that bolsters its own multiplication (self sustaining community). It serves to transmit bench marks and requirements throughout an assembly of people. The common unity holds, teaches, and evolves the tireless code of conduct for a working society. The coded imperatives, mission, and framework of our communities are the proverbial DNA of the formation.

1. It is the "we/they are this way because of" that elucidates the actual imperatives of a community and sheds light on the individual and group composition dynamics.

2. Norms that are conceived by us will work for us.

By now the need for an easy to embrace, but incremental, set of presiding laws should be clear. The need to ascertain a standard "go to" set of functional models while removing the confusion of where the starting points are for newcomers of higher sentience or group awareness are what we have addressed up until this point.

When composing the creed and ruling laws for the ANU Nation and ANU Life Global Ministries, we were presented with a similar demand. What principles could we subside on that allowed for adaptive engineering, when needed, but also retained a push towards alpha thought?

We resolved the difficulty applying the same theorization as mentioned above, proving that the best approach would be to look at principles already presented by our deep thought Ancestors and Elders. After auditing these principles for relevancy and efficacy, we moved forward with a schema that would address the intrinsic development of the individual and the external augmentation of the community, synchronously. The "14 Afrakan Principles" have not only brought lucidity to the community building undertakings but, have also been used in resolving family conflict, individual development, child rearing goal determinations, and even spiritual/social reclamation. It is a comprehensive account for judgement and checkpoints.

MAAT

CHIEF YUYA

Maat is a matured living reflection of cosmic morality. Cosmic morality differs with religious or ethical morality in that it does not cater to political or societal agenda. Cosmic morality is a righteous, harmonic wisdom that flows through an individual when they are erect in their character.

Maat is a nuclear prototype in the design of Nile Valley civilization philosophy and we witness her allusions in various pyramid texts. The Maat'ic principles protracted the very society of ancient Nile Valley civilization. Mastering her principles an individual was able to connect with the moving flow of cosmic blamelessness and channel the feminine energy of transformation through them.

We find accounts of Maat and her role in the "Pert Em HRU", which is often mistakenly called "The Book of the Dead". Albeit translating the title as "The Book of the Dead" is not far off from the Pert Em HRU's more accurate translation into English, which is "The Book of the Day", "The Book of Coming Forth by Day", or "The Book of the Sun". In denotation "Pert Em HRU" is asserting the *Book of Awakening* or the *Book of Transformation*. The metaphysical meaning of death is transformation. The laws of Maat are a part of a personal exercise of awakening into consciousness and transformation.

In the Pert Em HRU we find the 42 declarations, or confessions, of Maat. These confessions were found with variance, in other places such as entombment chambers of different individuals in Ta Meri (Ancient Egypt). Therefore, we learn through the varieties of the 42 negative confessions that the path of transformation is unique per the individual, as we all have our own karmic challenges to overcome. The seven central laws of Maat are, also, displayed with variance throughout the Nile Valley civilization. This reveals to us the Afrakan emphasis on metamorphosis and apropos dictum.

In this work we will look at the seven core keys of Maat as tools of inner transformation and awakening as opposed to a fixed set of rules. They are universal keys that unlock the way, or road, of unleashed consciousness in the adherent. **Note: When we are employing Afrakan deep thought wisdom we are interacting with holistic systems, primarily.** Maat is the feminine counterpart to the masculine force of Tehuti (Knowledge). In this, the keys that

Maat shares with us are to be carried out holistically and not to be taken out of context. Respect for the laws of gender must be upheld, as with all cosmic formulas, or the transforming alchemy of the formula is invalidated.

THE MAGIC OF MAAT

CHIEF YUYA

TRUTH

Truth does not necessarily reflect or collude with, perceptual realism. When we ask for the personal truth of another individual, typically, they will provide us with a chronological history of the thoughts/actions that led up to a certain decision or occurrence. Aside from that they can describe an action or thought that they may have chosen not to disclose, before. What is true is so elusive that it is hardly realized. Truth is the center of all in existence.

It should not be confused with fact. A fact is the aligning and agreeing to the majority conceptualization of reality or the larger acceptance of illusion which may, or may not, point to the truth.

Truth is matter in its actualized state. It is the soul of a force. All that exist around the truth is illusion. Illusion shrouds the potency of truth for those who have not developed the sensorium to witness the true forms of life and death, which are the materializations and disrobing of truth, respectively. We observe and experience truth's illusion through our five senses.

Our own physical bodies and mental/emotional structures are the illusions of the truth of the soul. As this great truth decides to form a vehicle suitable for the earth it forms genotypes through the manipulation of DNA which properly accommodate its intent.

The soul is the purest reflection of the truth that one could conceive of and even that conception cannot be grasped or even handled as its potency is too much for a flesh being. As truth is the undeniable essence of a force/person we can see that if a force has no soul, it has no truth. A soul is the eternal reflection of the high desire-less, causeless, intelligence we refer to as Akasha.

The truth is not static but, evolves as the laws of the universe do. Many will say that truth is forever. This is correct. The reason that it is eternal is because of its dynamic nature. That which stagnates in perfection and absoluteness will cease to be. *Keep it real/true, and live forever.*

The truth is what we responsibly petition when we feel we are strong enough to withstand a direct reverberation of Akashic energy. Akasha, as explained in the book "Shrine and Altar" is the substance, also known as "ether", that existed before all other elements (Earth, Fire, Water, Air, Metal) and gave birth to said elements. The phrase "baring the soul" comes to mind, here. When we bare our souls, we thrust aside the semblance of the body and the personality to allow the projection of our true drive, will, and intention to be observed. In order for one to comprehend this truth, they must first possess the truth inside them. Soul energy dispels artificial spirits as truth dispels false impression and judgement.

THE 14 KEYS
JUSTICE
Reward or punishment. Justice defines.

Just-Ice. To serve "just ice", would be a delivering of a stilling non-transforming demise. Due to this, we will use the term "even-handedness" as a healthier ANU interchange.

Justice is an administration of law. Law is the contour of a commanding order. In order for that law to be applicable to an individual, or group, the path/s to the supreme have to be wholeheartedly agreed on. There also must be an agreement on a calculation of law that holds jurisdiction over those who have contracted with it. Justice is a concept that invites great debate based on its inference to a changeable chain of command and rule of law.

As there are many ways of organizing an individual based on the contemplated values instilled from a divine rootage, there are many different laws. From person to person you may even find laws, or a sense of morality, that are contrasting in nature. This is not inherently problematic. Ultimately, one must do what works best towards the actualization of their pursuit. That mission will be defined and framed by the concept a person holds of their most supreme presence.

Equability differs from individual to individual. If there were one global assent on the nature of the divine and its place in the lives of those on earth, there would be only one law. This does not negate those time held principles that "we" consider to be ubiquitous. If we look across a span of societies, religions, and folk mores we will find certain principles that seem to live within, and at the core, of many different people.

At the source, the aim of justice/even-handedness should be peace. Peace is one of the most universal concepts incarnate in the ambition of all beings on the planet. Peace is not synonymous with serenity but rather, is more closely related to character identification.

In a society bent on arresting the development and growth of natural incarnate beings, a new debauched sense of "justice" becomes the operating prerequisite.

Even-handedness is a means of directing individuals towards what would relatively be considered high morality. For example, if one says, "Cleanliness is next to godliness" the conclusion would infer that a "clean" person is closer to the highest authority in all existence than an unclean one. Would the same be deduced for organisms that thrive and develop in unhygienic environments? Would they serve a different "creator" or would their justice/even-handedness be characteristic to their biological environment? This demonstrates the changing relativity of justice's judgement.

Even-handedness provides the rewards and punishments associated with discriminating actions. It is the method that the cause and effect axiom are delivered through. This idea of cause and effect, or give and take, connect us to the Maat'ic concept of reciprocity.

Through our acceptance of rewards and punishments we accept external definition. The type of reciprocal cause and effect that we experience becomes the character of, not only our reciprocity but also, our supreme reality.

RECIPROCITY

Reciprocity is the act of giving back, directly to the original sender, what has been given. In reality, it is inconceivable for one to return exactly what has been sent to them due to ever-changing internal/external variables. So what is returned is always a best effort of the returnee. For example, because the mobility of time is continual each moment of existence is changing. The ideation, force, and element that comprises what we would send differs from moment to moment in the same way *we* differ from moment to moment. This means that reciprocity is the exchange of inter-meshed, but not equivalent, forces. We can draw from the adage, "You can never step in the same stream twice".

Love is the embryonic draw of reciprocal exchange. In fact, love and reciprocity are practically synonymous. When there is a reciprocal exchange, one force must be the giver while the other is the receiver, and vice versa. Love is the article that connects forces of opposite polarities together. In order for reciprocity to "work" there must be a desire to affix entities that are seemingly on the diametric polarity spectrum. This formulates an interlocking.

Reciprocity animates and sustains the hardiness of an individual. Without give and take there is no human life. We conserve our life by inhalation and exhalation. Enlarging this idea beyond the body sphere, we can see this same interplay at work inside a community paradigm. It is the exchange of energy within a community that braces its members and provides for a reaffirming of the guiding mission and core doctrine of the group. Reciprocity is the metabolic breath of a group or community.

Through our give and take we establish our own refining system. As we dispense energy, thoughts, feelings, and resources among each other we tend to filter out the elements that do not work for where we are aiming. This is why it is important to reflect on the highest *and* lowest ideas that we share among one another. This enables us to see what we are caching into our environments, and selves.

Each component that compiles what we comprehend ourselves to be are continually giving to us, while our encounters with the world are taking away from those very same factors in us. Our internal environment mirrors and generates the bilateral push and pull that we witness throughout the multiverse. Reciprocity is the pulsating breath that expels what we no longer need and intakes what we long to be.

When we give, we create living forms of our negated selves through the very imprint of our endowments. Consider our giving/offering as an exhalation. When exhaling we motivate the breath of life or spirit. All that we attest and offer outwards into the world is a form of exhaled spirit. The spirits we create are negated constructs of our own soul or psyche (no different from the *human* creation being a negated form of a more supreme force). The spirits we give/exhale saturate the objects we send out into the world, like polymerized clones of our own thoughts. This is one half of the reciprocal process.

Inspire means to be "in spirit". "Spire" is a root form of the word "spiral" and "spirit". The word spirit means "breath". To take "in" spirit is to take in breath. Our inhalations are a means of inspiration. When we receive we are ingesting spirit in many contrasting forms. We have just discussed that an exhalation/offering is impregnated with spirit. So when we receive something, or someone, we are in-taking spirit. In others words we are being "inspired". Reception is a means of enlivening. Silence and death receive life to recycle the life force again.

The constant pulsation of reciprocity intends life. Via reciprocity the self transfers itself into the subject. Producing a likeness of ourselves is evidence of a perfecting of the fineness of our present state. When this process stops, annihilation ensues.

THE 14 KEYS
HARMONY

The vibratory contracts made to compose what we call "reality" are the nuclear basis of harmony. Our experiences are comprised of a series of contracts that interweave among truth and illusion or non-being and being.

Harmony is a designed tapestry of differing vibrations to construct an idyllic blend. This cosmic phenomena requires diversified vibrations. The stipulation of diversity does not negate from the importance of comporting in unison but, harmony takes into account the uniqueness of complex forces and concepts and finds a point at which they can converge and complement each others crux.

This can happen between any given number of units. For this work we should remember that individuals and groups are "units" that carry their own vibratory tone autonomously and corporately.

What we call "music" is a harmonic blend of sound and silence.

A body in its natural state of health is in harmony with itself and its holding environment. When a force is in harmony with the natural environment it protracts itself via a reciprocal exchange of energy. A force that is out of harmony with itself, will also be out of harmony with its contextual environment. In fact, it may find itself in an environment that is not designed for its own native vibration. When this harmonic dislocation happens, it experiences discord.

The only way to resolve this discord is to change the cooperative design to adhere to the fallible vibration/tone/unit/person or remove that vibration/tone/unit/person from the, otherwise, agreeable composition.

"One bad apple can spoil the bunch".

One errant vibration can knock the entire arrangement out of harmonic alignment and atomize the integrity of the grouping.

If an energy is where it does not belong it becomes unable to sustain itself through the natural complementary process of giving and receiving, organically, with its surroundings. When this displacement is present either the environment will feed disproportionately from said energy or the energy will take its food from the environment, as opposed to exchanging energy with it.

As we sink deeper into the catatonic caverns of our own ego, the likelihood for euphonious placement within any environment, other than the one charted by our own egocentric thoughts, becomes less and less likely. When this happens we find ourselves constantly searching for a place where we can feel like we belong. The isolating effect of our internal disharmony becomes more apparent as the natural defense mechanisms of the universe protects others from our dis-eased state of being.

The universe will insure that mutation or dissolution occurs in a banished space as not to interfere with the journey of others on this long red road of life.

When the ego takes over, completely, we convince ourselves that we are so special that the problem is with the world and its inhabitants as we are resolute in our point of view. Our own defective personality/vibratory emission never comes into question.

Denial is a great place to live, if you can afford the rent. The price to pay is barrenness.

THE 14 KEYS

BALANCE

Balance is the indispensable charge of a human life. It is knowing our place in the quantum field. Balance is regularity across the horizontal and vertical plane. The horizontal is the principle of the world. The vertical concept is the idea of the divine.

The symbolic heart is the fulcrum point between the land above the planar and the land below it. At the heart we make determinations as to whether we will aspire towards the mortal life or the cherubic life. We own a consciousness in the heavens and a consciousness on earth. Each one compels attention, maintenance, and unremitting linkage with the other to maintain a straight line across the unapparent life course.

The horizontal illustrates our journey through the world of human life. The horizontal concept reinforces the cognition that we are equal with all in creation. We strive to complete our internal acts of goodness so that we can see ourselves as finished beings. The idea of "oneness" is a product of this leveling concept. Working from the horizontal dimension imparts a sense that there is no descension or ascension, there is no supernatural vs. natural, and nature is conjoined with all reality on the equilateral plane. The unseen world does not exist beneath or above the individual but, rather alongside.

The vertical concept, in balance, approximates the procession toward power as the horizontal is a movement towards beauty. The vertical infers hierarchy and a distinction between the ordinary and extraordinary. True power is acquired from the world of the unseen. In that, the vertical represents the transmission of power. The horizontal concept represents a state of impotence.

Analogous to the aperture of the longitudinal expression of the female sexual cove, we behold the entrance to power. However, the vertical concept is closely associated with the day and the sun while the horizontal, the moon and night So, we find complementary symmetry present in the spatial dimensions of the horizontal day and the vertical night.

The vertical causes us to look towards the uprightness of a properly aligned spine and its fundamental relationship to character. As character formatively descends on an individual from a celestial prelude, it is the reconnecting with that source that cultivates and polishes that same stature. Here we behold a greater measure of the word "nurture". It is the nurturing/"naturing" that we receive from the feminine/motherly/vertical principle which helps to contour our character. This nurturing helps us to straighten our proverbial spine and to live with character uprightly, as defined by our Most High.

To achieve a state of balance all parts in any given order must receive their precise portion of energy so that none are wanting or stockpiling excess energy units. An internal system functions on compositions of self reliance, as well. Your own body feeds from itself and has a series of interdependent parts. When one of these parts are working harder to compensate for the failure of another, then can sickness occur. Internal malady is a by-product of an internal imbalance.

The imbalance that spreads contamination throughout an organism always dawns in the orbit of spirit. When there is a misconception of a spiritual need, based on the acceptance of a deficit model, the neglected component becomes the basis of imbalance throughout the organism. For example, when one is unaware of their spiritual body, as a whole, they tend to invest more in the ephemeral human body. When that becomes the primary investment, the mainlines to nourishment for the spirit are blocked by the deluded mind (*"The mind is the gateway to all spiritual experiences" - Grasping the Root of Divine Power*). With this scenario, an imbalance develops wherein it requires the spirit to forage outside itself for nutrition and the body loses its guidance system and agency in the spirit world. This manifest itself in the need for constant sacramental sacrifice of other organisms, a falsified sense of self, a lack of ancestral/spiritual support, and a sense of muddiness as to what life after death needs in preparation.

Balance is a term that usually is more pointed than the assertion of the idea of "fairness". When balance is present, a body has the ability to supply the needs of its own demands without annexing extraneous subsidy. Spiritual and physical organisms, in balance, sustain each other via the interchanging of each others energy. When there is an imbalance present, those corporeal/celestial bodies must seek outside themselves to provide the sustenance needed.

THE 14 KEYS
ORDER

Order is a procedure of arrangement. It is the differentiation and compartmentalization of higher energy into lower energy. Consider the process of narrowing and converging a collection of thoughts into a single idea. The thoughts would cast a form of countless feasibility because they have not yet been rallied into an action. Once the thought/high energy is focused into a physical action/lower energy that action, or physical embodiment, will be imbued with only the determined idea. This is one reason meditation is so arduous for some. When one decides to observe mental trajectories, they are viewing the recurrent thought traffic that occurs in the mind before unfolding.

Establishing order incorporates the consignment of the divine creative spirit. The creative essence is chaotic in nature. Its amorphousness gives all the ore for conception we need to bring forth the meant forces of creation. Chaos is the stimulus for creativity. Once creation occurs chaos gives way to defined order. Those "defined" forces are what we discern as life and existence.

Order defines the feminine chaos. Order is masculine in character. Both are needed to begin the enterprise we call "life". Before order, the unceasing movement of energy is random and distends into the nonexistence of the abyss. It is boundless and has no orientation of position. Once a call for definition is placed into the void (light discharged into darkness), the chaotic energy will condense and slow its vibratory rate. Particles begin to slow up and form shapes. These shapes are what make up what we perceive to be our mental, then physical factuality.

Order is a stilling of neuro-spiritual particles. When we establish order, we are establishing definitions. Those definitions can grow and clarify themselves from their point of fabrication because until they reach their apex of existence they are still condensing. To simplify, consider the journey of a child to an adult, to an Elder. There is a journey from thought, to soft flesh, to harder flesh, back to soft flesh and then an eventual dissipation of atoms again.

CHIEF YUYA

When order is established infinite possibility is cropped into the path of creation. Order is a slenderizing of the road or a tightening down of the determinations in front of us. As mentioned before, truth is at the centrality of our existence. Once creation is formed figment takes the place of the truth of indistinctness. The five senses conceal that encased life, in reality, is counterfeit. The actual essence of a force/thing is the truth. Once definition befalls, that essence is buckled in a veil of order. This is not to say that order is a detrimental thing. Order helps us to define and question our potential.

As we are living in a spiritual world alongside a physical one, it is important for us to invest in the freedom of chaos and also rejoice in the balance that comes from physical order. Physical order is necessary to establish unity. Through order we redefine the many demonstrations of all working parts. Ordering our brain works and categorizing the spiritual energy around us is necessary for us even to intend ourselves. The order that exists around us, or lack thereof, reveals the current level of mastery we have above our minds. The more we can order our thoughts, the greater our productive potency.

RIGHTEOUSNESS

Righteousness is the act of being functionally relevant within the current perceptual context. *Our codes of righteousness should be certified by the needs and policies required for our liberation.* Propriety/Righteousness is not akin to morality, which is usually offered up through religious dogmatic indoctrination.

Example: **Swearing on the bible.** *Swearing on the bible only means something to one who appraises the bible a sacred object. In the Ogun state of Nigeria, individuals going through a legal process pledge their affirmations on a piece of iron.*

In these examples we see propriety is linked with personal devotion to something considered sacred, as prescribed by a larger social architecture.

Our commencing environment is the maternal womb. From there, the enclosure expands outwards to our kinship consciousness and then cyclically reciprocates back into a perception of self. Each environment requires a code of governance which allows the dweller to *best* take advantage of the laws that govern that environment. So, for example, righteousness within the internal body awareness would display the law and ideal spirit of the body. We, typically, refer to this as "*good health*". If what you are doing is not working towards the crowning notions of an approved contract within an environment, it is unrighteous.

Righteousness compels us to do what is right. However, "right and wrong" are subjective particularities depending on the social or personal concern of an individual. Righteousness is just as subjective as the idea of "good".

Performing righteous/unrighteous acts engenders karma. The karmic cycle compels one to engage their environment via some form of deed. No matter the intention of the initiator, the action will dualistically fall into the act of righteous or unrighteous.

The artist Nas once said, "I exhale the yellow smoke of Buddha through righteous steps" in his song "It ain't hard to tell". Additionally, we read, in, the book known as "The Holy Bible" Psalm 37:23, "The steps of a good man are ordered by the LORD". The very footsteps of an individual can be considered right or wrong depending on the affect they have on the fulfillment of said individuals destiny and their surroundings. A turn to the left or the right can set off a series of events that either lead a person farther along the path of their purpose or could lead them on a decade long digression.

Proprietary/Righteousness, itself, is an active universal organism that finds nature in the embodiment of the given moment. Reformation is its means of survival.

Truth is an evolving presence. When truth seeks out the exhibition of its own level, in any given moment, it offers its wisdom to the individual as "righteousness". When an individual is filled with the deified power known as truth, they become righteous. The power of truth is revealed on a personal level by the living of its doctrine and commandments.

Righteousness can be defined by the infill and living of the spiritual truth. If truth provides the light that navigates one to their highest purpose, then righteousness can be the abiding light within an individual. To be righteous is to be completed with light. This light helps to provide directional agency and is not, within itself, the truth. Knowledge is not enough. Knowledge must stand inside of the seeker (Innerstanding).

It should be innerstood that all the afore mentioned concepts are alterable and subject to the soul of the ascribed context.

THE 14 KEYS

NGUZO SABA

CHIEF YUYA

THE 14 KEYS

From Dr. Karenga:

"The Nguzo Saba are the moral minimum value system Black people need in order to rescue and reconstruct their history and humanity, indeed their daily lives, in their own image and interests."

The name Kwanzaa comes from a phrase of Swahili origin, "Matunda Ya Kwanza", and translates as "First Fruits of the Harvest".

In this work we are focusing on the seven principles as undertaken by the Kawaida faith and channeled through Dr. Maulana Karenga and the US organization. Our focus will not be on the celebration of Kwanzaa, its apparatuses, or the profound impact the harvest celebration has had on Afrakans throughout the world.

Dr. Karenga is a capable lecturer with a confirmed account of community contract since the 1960's. According to Karenga, he developed the holiday known as Kwanzaa to provide a moral, cultural, and social orientation for black people worldwide which would attach them to a pan African design process.

The principles of Kwanzaa, known as the Nguzo Saba, provide a framework for an ongoing struggle to transform the self concept of disenfranchised Afrakans domestically and abroad. The commandments outlined in the seven principles of Kwanzaa provide an active command to those who have embraced the celebration and responsibility. With each principle there are the words "struggle" or "strive" used to accentuate the ongoing work that is required to bring the achievement of the higher vision of the holiday and philosophy to fruition.

Dr. Karenga has provided a splendid model that illustrates the ongoing synthesis of new concepts required to fulfill the promise of Afrakan liberation. The Nguzo Saba is neither a complete model for social or personal reclamation but, provides the mapping that one needs to draft their work. Utilizing these sacred principles also helps one to discern if what they are investing in is constructing a healthier commonwealth or unhinging the sacred task of the nation builder.

CHIEF YUYA

UMOJA (UNITY)

"To strive for and maintain unity in the family, community, nation and race."

Unity is alignment with one mission and pulse. Unity develops consonance when aiming towards a single target as a group. The group, itself, does not require assimilation of duty between all members but, in fact, is a medley of diversified forces working in collusion with one another.

Unity is a location, not a conceptual inseparability or a sense of camaraderie among individuals. Individual forces build this place, known as unity, by functioning in their **authorized** roles over a period of time.

Similar to a living body, unity is built by laboring, not just asserting, towards a single purpose. Unity is not achieved by, merely, claiming togetherness or demanding it. It is acquired through work and cooperation between partnering constituents.

These solitary forces are charged by an archetypal head that bestows the mission and orders for the total organism. Each organism has a commission of that "head" within it so, they are all bonded by this bio/spiritual kinship. The cells in a body mirror this same idea. Each cell in a body has a brain center of its own but, is launched by the impulses and directives of the central brain unit (the head).

Looking at this from a religious/spiritual perspective, there are many streams of consciousness that emit from a central god-head. In polymorphic traditions these streams are called by many names from Angels, Orisha, Loa, Neteru, Nkisi, Abosom, and more. This family of multiple streams all act within a different dimension of consciousness but are apart of the same realm of creation. Through their activation and implementation a united spiritual kingdom is created. They all share the creative makeup of their pattern designer but, work in tandem with different faculties and unique nature to fulfill the mission of the hierarchical creator intelligence.

Strength is shared between the members of a family, community, nation, and race by way of sympathy. Sympathy is the act of sharing or communing a specific feeling. When we assemble ourselves and share the details of our work with each other we are able to share the emotion (energy in motion) that the work has invoked in us. By, sharing this emotion we share energy among our constituents. Once this energy is served, those we are partnered with should respond with support and innerstanding. For example, it is commonly noted that when one loses one of their natural faculties that another inward faculty will increase in power and strength to compensate for the loss of one of its working parts. Also, we often find incidents where one may develop a physical problem in one part of their body that is attempting to compensate for another part of their body that is ailing and unable to perform its job to proper functional capacity. To further clarify, one may have an issue with their right leg and, without thinking, begin to put more weight on their left leg. The body automatically has a sympathetic reaction to the right leg and distributes strength to it for healing while also compensating for its decline in function so the entire organism can continue to comport as directed by the brain.

The head is critical in forming the refuge known as unity. It holds the operating system that coordinates the functions of the groups matrix. This is often called a mission. Without a mission, unity can be used as a weapon of genocide. When individuals are building singleness under the orders of a foreign/subversive command, collapse will soon follow. We persevere by the precedence we are created from. When we attempt to take orders from a foreign intelligence that does not contain the same creation matter flowing through our own being, we are being charged with foreign toxins. This is no different from using processed, artificial, foods to acquire your sustenance. These foods are counterfeit and therefore they do not support your natural bodily functions and state of health. Toxic foods sustain the toxic aspects of ourselves. We must be directed by those who share our same Creators' essence.

CHIEF YUYA

KUJICHAGULIA (SELF-DETERMINATION)
"To define ourselves, name ourselves, create for ourselves and speak for ourselves."

Kujichagulia is one of the most consequential principles for the consciously aware.

When we look at the various charges of self-determination, as outlined by Maulana Karenga, we first see the commission to define ourselves. With that call for self-defining behaviors and self-defining initiatives let us take a look at what definition means in the mind and heart of the culture builder. To define something is to substantiate an ending point and boundary for that which is being defined. In being self-defining, we certify what our own end points are, as well as our own limitations. When we say that we are self-defining and we choose what our lives will be, we install the edges where our lives can proceed to and when our personal lines end. Boundaries can be stretched and they can be manipulated. If we are not the ones who established our boundaries to begin with then we certainly will not be the ones who will be able to move them or expand them at will. We can only live within foreign boundaries, or escape them. Self-defining is a process of determining our own limitations and our own destinations.

We cannot be swayed and influenced by alien forces.

A question that is commonly asked is, "What is in a name?". A name is a vital fraction to one's own self actualization. When we choose to be self-determined, self-defining, and self-actualizing the first thing that we do is establish a titled attribute or call of command that will cast us into a lofty idea of being. A name is a continual and durable charge that can limit or expand one's energetic matrix.

Names define forces for external and individual processing. A title can bring out the highest value or it can subdue the greater value in a force. Each name that one is given, or one takes on for themselves, has a decisive syllabic value and frequency resonance. It is through sound frequency that we invoke spirits. So each time we accept a name for ourselves we are, in fact, invoking a certain spirit within ourselves.

The sound current oscillation of your name should always vibrate and rise out to the highest idea of your own defined bound-

42

ary. Your name should reach out through acoustics and reverberation to whatever it is that you conceive to be your highest power and pull the characteristics that are paramount within your potential down to you. Extracting a characteristic from a very deep and unseen place is a personal invocation. Names and titles have an unseen secret power to do this.

Names/titles define forces. Once we are able to name a force, we are able to gain knowledge of it. It it through this knowing that we are able to gain a mastery of it. We cannot command that which we have no knowledge of. Labeling ourselves is a step towards knowing ourselves and, ultimately, ruling ourselves.

When we review the notion of creating and speaking for ourselves it is useful to think of the power of conscious creation. Creation is a gapless process. There are many different articles that go into the creating of a person, or a community. A community, or group, is not just created through an issued proclamation. A community, or a group, is created through a conscious unfurling of all the elements that were present when the group first was envisioned in one's mind. Conscious creation begins with the **consciousness**. There must be a design and construction process that occurs in the conscious mind before it occurs in the physical. If this does not happen, then one is creating dis-harmoniously. Without putting the correct emphasis on our divine call to create consciously, we manufacture a reality that brings discord and disease. Regardless of our desire to create or speak for ourselves, we are flatly doing it anyway. The culture and habits that we invest in are our silent statement. If we are not generating a culture for ourselves through coefficient self determination we are in fact, creating unconsciously and likely following the inventive cultural designs of a disaffiliated consciousness.

Thoughts create our reality through the ore of mental matter. Our thoughts commission emotion. These passions actuate energy to later form into what we view as our reality.

We must define ourselves through the impression of our higher consciousness and not the pull of our lower sense conventionality. Our higher consciousness instills itself into our group awareness. Outside of that, we define using the ego. The ego seeks for boundaries out of fear, as opposed to evolution. It is fear that blocks the paths to self determination because fear instills the notion of a feasible loss of "power". Being ourselves can be seen as an act of aggression. True power is internal, not external so, the fear of a loss of it, within itself, is a farce.

Truth is the essence that lives in our souls, which directs our consciousness. Our groups must contain the corner stone of truth to provide a standard of behavior and mission template for its members. This means each member must be a curator and discoverer of rightness. When that truth animates within each group member, it creates a true cohesiveness and ambition of Kujichagulia.

"To control a people you must first control what they think about themselves and how they regard their history and culture. And when your conqueror makes you ashamed of your culture and your history, he needs no prison walls and no chains to hold you." - **Dr. John Henrik Clarke**

UJIMA (COLLECTIVE WORK AND RESPONSIBILITY)

"To build and maintain our community together and make our brother's and sister's problems our problems and to solve them together."

Collective work and responsibility calls for compassion of the highest order. The best self preservation that one could achieve is the preservation that comes at the behest of group preservation. Compassion becomes the medium for sharing energy and strength between those who are engaged in a common struggle. When we engage in the operation of community rearing or citizenry formulating, each individual involved must do the work that supports the collective and the work that suits their natural faculties and merited aptitudes.

Our existence cannot be sustained outside of the overlapping factors and coalitions that make up what we call the *greater family*. These overlapping components act interdependently for the purposes of community sustainability. Pursuits of personal interest pale in comparison to the prospective that individual liberties are upheld by the cooperative institutions that assign a sense of group esteem, self respect, and security of covering.

A responsive culture is needed in order to fashion the skills of self-governance that one must use to conduct themselves, as well as a civic-minded sense of group service. Communities must have the ability to respond to the needs of the individuals and adapt the appropriate changes required in order to maintain and protect the mental, spiritual, physical, and social health of its members. This becomes the collective work and responsibility of the community, itself.

Moral, legal, and social issues are the referenced check points when one is making long-term decisions within a community. Collective work and responsibility direct one to think about what is needed to maintain the ecological fitness of the family structure, morality of the group, its ethos, and the choices that create the long term ripple effects throughout the social organism.

Often there may exist communities inside communities that

comprise a collective organism. Due to this, it is important that the moral perspective of one group never be held over another but, allowed to be judged by external criteria that speak to the values expected to advance and arrange the human experience per the celestial directive.

Decorous principles are first anchored in the home. Bringing children (returning ancestors) into the world requires, not only, articles of material sustenance but, also a restorative instilling of cosmic morality. Implanting morals and culture within OUR children require close bonding. It is not enough to leave this work to educators, child care providers, or religious institutions. In light of this we must be *close bonded*, as a community, to partake in the valued and esteemed roles as parents. This responsibility and task go beyond the nuclear family. In this, our brothers and sisters challenges (problems) become our own. Their children become our children and the obligation of reinforcing correct acclimation and self pride becomes the common work. **Note: This should not be used as a parachute for those who choose to create children irresponsibly or premeditate single parent households. The gravity of OUR chronicled, sociological, and intellectual data suggest that most often two-parent homesteads fair better at executing their child-raising duties based on healthy cultural models and if for no reason other than there being four hands to help as opposed to two.**

Collective rights of passage help us to identify those who are seriously prepared about the work that is awaited of all members of a given society. In order for us to respond properly with ability in any group setting to achieve our goals, there must be a system of rites of passage to determine who is qualified to do what. These Rites of Passage also account participants to the watchful eye and expectations of the communities that they are authenticated in front of, publicly. Once this is done there is a common agreement between those who have been initiated into assorted functions of the community as to what the guiding mission is and their role in fulfilling it. Ujima not only calls for us to become one another's keepers but, also calls for us to enforce collective policies across the board. For example, if someone is known to be a traitor to their people Ujima calls us to shun them and inform our love ones of the potential danger they present. Far too often, community building efforts are undermined by a lack of coactive policy and moral principle. Individuals can, and often do, collectively work and respond with ability to create anarchism, disease, and further fuel death culture. Of course, this can be done haphazardly, and unconsciously. It is important for us to know the value of our collective work and to prove to those who would depend on us whether it be in an enlarged community setting, or a family setting, that we have the proven acumen to respond with **ability**.

CHIEF YUYA

UJAMAA (COOPERATIVE ECONOMICS)

"To build and maintain our own stores, shops and other businesses and to profit from them together."

Cooperative economics are economics that work together. Strictly sharing resources and cash between members of a society or group does not constitute cooperative economics. The actual goods and services must also perform interdependently to construct a self sustaining economic web. Therefore, the "cooperative" in "cooperative economics" is not just about individuals in receipt of financial bank notes, providers of services, or purveyors of goods conducting transaction with one another. Cooperative economics provides a means for the very goods and services to serve one another. For example, if a given community specializes in the creation of paper goods, it would benefit that community additionally to instate a transportation service to haul those goods. This same community might establish sufficient fueling and service stations for these vehicles. In this scenario each economic component establishes a relationship with one another that synchronously supports the entire structure, as well as themselves.

Our economics are the goods and services that sustain our lives. "Eco" means "life" or "the home". "Nomo/s" means "to manage". *Economics* is the management of our homes, lives, and establishment of sustaining homes in joint fashion.

The home is a representation of our will and spiritual expenditure. At times you will hear different religious organizations referred to as the "house of...". Such as the "House of Israel" or "The House of Judah". The house represents what a person is actually doing and what feeds them, as well as where their installment is. So to sustain and manage one's own house, is to continue and control one's own will. The house, or home, as a representation of the human will also becomes a depiction of the human mind. The house is an expression of one's wisdom, knowledge, and spiritual telepathy. There is a direct connection between the way we observe economics and the way we discern the owning of our own intellectual property. An empty house can be allegorized to an empty mind. An empty mind is an impoverished one, affixed to an economically desolate individual.

The house, or homestead, can also comparatively relate to our bodies. Our houses are the shelters and abode of the living spirit. In some instances we even refer to the house, or body, as the "temple". There is a sacred indication inherent in the concept of a house, or homestead, that reaches beyond the notion of a mere physical shelter.

If we do not control the mechanisms that back our homesteads, we can deduce that we do not administer our lives or minds. Co-operative economics, not only designs a pathway for the flow of currency but also, cultivates the symbiotic relationships needed for controlling the life of our community.

Cooperative economics cannot be executed within a vacuum or on a lone farm in the countryside but, calls for us to spend among those who are about our mission, cause, and plan. An economy does not begin when one is in receipt of "money". An economy originates with the acknowledgment of the relationships that exist among a group of people. In fact, one does not need financial bank notes in order to establish an economy. One needs to first establish the working relationships among a collective to determine the nature and goals of that economy.

For example, water distribution is a viable mode of economic transference which typically does not need to involve the exchange of minted currency.

One could free trade services as a means of economic union.

In order for an economy to reside upon the very bonds of the members of a community, those members of that community must participate in close bonding experiences that bring about a healthy sense of togetherness. One cannot establish a cultural, or even ethnic, economy from a distance. There must be a collective objective substantiated first. That collective quest typically provides the transference of communal mores, principles, and ethnic dictum. **For example: bartering hair braiding services for baby sitting services is a suitable example of synergistic economics.**

CHIEF YUYA

In order to know who is qualified to braid hair or provide child care services one must first know the members of their community.

Interesting enough, when one visits communities that actually have created kinship like relationships among its members, you will find that the nature of "haggling" is very aggressive. There is no shame in negotiation among friends. The wealth and goods are being shared among people who are kin-like. When there is an abstraction of economy financial transactions are frosty, mutually unfruitful, and the relationships formed from them are distanced by the spirit that is central in the currency used. The spirit of the currency is an active projection of the minters who first placed value on it.

Cooperative economics are economics that work in the best good of the actual economic/life management ambition. The economy is the governance of the life and minds of the members of said economy. So in order for a healthy economy to be residing there must be an ambition to initiate healthy cerebration. Intelligence, wisdom, and moralistic values must be high on the priority chart of all members of that community. This is where cooperative economics begins and economic exploitation halts.

Maintenance of the life and home takes into account future and past generations. It does not reset with the fiscal year or when quarterly objectives are met.

THE 14 KEYS
NIA (PURPOSE)

"To make our collective vocation the building and developing of our community in order to restore our people to their traditional greatness."

Purpose is the piloting principle that looms over the heads of all human beings like a cloud formation. Purpose causes us to analyze our lives. Many choose to disregard the proverbial overhead question mark that we are all born with and opt to live an "unexamined life".

What we endeavor to do in any given moment is only disclosed when we inject the fullness of our being and divine sensation into the "Now". This is how we begin to experience transcendental moments. Transcendental moments are those experiences that we have in life, that lead us to a total shattering of our current perceptual reality. For some, it is a gargantuan woeful event and for others it may be something as minute and negligible as a flower growing out of a concrete sidewalk.

When the divine enters a human experience, the divine seeks to amplify the experience to its rims. This expansion is what we call growth and evolution. If we envision ourselves to be divine beings, as created in the image of a divine intelligence containing like elements of that intelligence, then our purpose will always be to elongate the restrictions of evolution that exists within the cell of every conjuncture. In order to do this, we must be amenable to the innate fascination of the in/out-dwelling personality we call "God" and its revolution.

The crux of our existence reveals itself by way of inquisition, exploration, speculation, and faith. The capability to sense the full nature of each moment of our lives, becomes the amazing competence that allows us to know what to be in those moments. This is, in itself, a divine endowment. There are many who walk the earth who have no sense of timing or of what the moment calls for. In some instances we call the presence of that gift, "social skills" or "situational awareness".

Our purpose is to be fully present during all metamorphic experiences. This obligates us to be totally receptive to what is being shared with us by all forces that comprise the moment, and then to examine the meaning of the moment with our finite reasoning faculties. Our minds are constantly expanding as, the mind is the celestial counterpart of the human brain. The celestial heavens expand based on the growing wonders of humanity.

With the above being said, we soon realize that purpose is dynamic. Human reality, and even the mortal creation, is flawed from its very emergence. We find evidence of this through the creation tales of various religious and spiritual systems, especially those that are connected to the African continent. In the error and fallibility we develop the spirit of questioning. It is in the vacillation between speculation and acceptance that we discover purpose. Our purpose is the premier question the heavenly self has of itself that it can neither ask nor answer in its perfected form.

For nation builders each moment is a transcendental one. Every decision we are faced with has long-term rippling effect in regards to how it will affect the waves of generations that follow the work we perform. With the absorption of the moment, as divine beings, we must search to discover if the moment brings balance to our lives or if it further sends us out of alignment. At times, our purpose will be to reconstitute the principles and laws of balance that govern a single moment or an expansive dispensation of time.

The divine Nia for each individual is unique and customized per individual and never dependent or inclusive of others despite what we perceive as the dignity of our life purposes. We travel through life experiencing what we create based on the thoughts that we offer most our attention to. As our thoughts change, our creative potential changes. As our creative potential changes our life reality changes. As all these components are altering, the nature of our questions are also changing. This means the dynamic statement of our own purpose begins to evolve.

We all have a purpose. It is a grave error to live a life without examination and inquisition. There is often a curiosity with the ending of our realities. Of course, this interest revolves around the fear of our current framework of existence ending. Some refer to this moment and event as "death". So to distract oneself from this obsession, individuals will pursue interests that seem purposeful and significant but, intentionally, do not answer the innate questions. These diversions even birth durational religions. They germinate opiate based gospels wherein the ultimate goal is feeling good. The truth is, owning a purpose and absorbing the moment can feel so wretched at times that the reality of one's existence becomes painfully undeniable.

Many host a paralyzing fear surrounding the idea that if the primal core questions are answered then, life will cease to be. There is a truth in this. Life as we know it ceases to be when we reach the plateau of comprehending our actual purpose.

The principle of Nia causes us to look at the solutions and lifestyles that are suitable to our circumstance so, we can create a formation which reflects the call of Kujichagulia.

CHIEF YUYA
KUUMBA (CREATIVITY)
"To do always as much as we can, in the way we can, in order to leave our community more beautiful and beneficial than we inherited it."

In the continuous movement called "creativity", divine matter has chosen a single path of travel. Divine thought matter is in flux and has chosen to pursue a singular channel of incarnation. This marks the transition of potential to creation. Kuumba is consciousness in motion.

Creation is an ongoing process. The lower world is created, rightly, as the high nature is perceived. Life as we know it is not a container of predestined substances that we are granted the opportunity to experience. Life unfolds as we crave it to. This does not rule out the divine orchestration of chosen destiny but, how we respond to that destiny and the choices we make create the life we experience.

If we compare ourselves with the vastness of the universe we seem to be small, and possibly even insignificant, members of the life continuum. However, we do have the possibility for colossal impact on this planet. Earth is the chosen realm of transformation which has materialized for our discovery. Here, we have created a planet-wide testing center for our souls.

When we look at the various creation stories offered to us by way of ancient indigenous, and even contemporary western, traditions we find the responsibility of human creation discharged to an entity who fails at recreating the perfection found in the heavens. Plant life, animal life, marine life, nor mineral life seems to reflect the failure of the craftsmen/wombmyn of creation but, we are constantly reminded of the inherent flaw of man's creation.

The planted defect in human design becomes an important factor when we choose to further develop as humanity, and even from our five human senses. Once it is realized that human creation is flawed from its manifestation, and not its conception, we glean that the flaws within ourselves and our constructions are divine occurrences. Many of us spend lifetimes attempting to create a better world, or to create a progressive model of mankind. If we are reflections of a higher, older, more evolved intelligence and that matriarchal / patriarchal power created us in error and flaw then it would stand to reason that whatever we create will also be filled with inwoven errors and flaws. This becomes significant when we reflect on our lives and the egotistical conviction that comes so easily at times because we rail against errors that are naturally occurring and will always natively be present. If human creation is blemished, what humans create will also be flawed. Any force that travels from its pure potential to a state of condensed order will contain flaws.

In light of the previously stated data, origination now takes on a meaning that may seem dissimilar than what recent learning traditions has imparted to us. Creation is a never ending casting of high functioning spiritual potential energy. The fast moving energy that exist before creative order is "chaos". In order to create this order, this energy must be slowed down enough to be controlled. Once chaos is bridled, it becomes imperfect. Part of its incompleteness lies in its new definition. Chaos is a substance from the primordial pools of undifferentiated matter. It is perfect because it is unchanging, wants for nothing, and lacks the definition of judgement. This perfection is cessation. That what does not change, does not grow. That which does not grow crystallizes in one dimension of reality. If, and when, that dimension changes or ends, then that which has not grown beyond it ends, as well. We must creatively evolve.

The growth of the consciousness of humanity enriches the interdimensional plain. Human beings can be likened to escape pods or life rafts sent from the Mother Ship known as "God". These life rafts or escape pods have the mission to seek out new life. To discover new life the passengers of these vessels must discern and perceive their existence differently than they did before. If they saw exactly as they did before in their perfected state, they would be unable to see the different dimensions of life and existence that could potentially be. This is a macroscopic representation of the perils of the human ego.

Ironically, the masses of humanity are often obsessed with life that exist beyond planet earth and even send ships into the vast reaches of outer space in order to discover that which would be "new" to them. The truth is, that which is new unfolds on the "Plan-et". A "plan" is a proposed method of achieving an intended goal. The suffix "et" specifies a diminishing of the root concept of a word. So, the "planet" is the smaller plan. On the planet, we are reflecting and living out a negated facsimile of a higher plan, unrealized.

Our creativity mirrors a loftier fore*thought*. When we are not mirroring that higher intention, we run the risk of creating unconsciously. Unconscious creation occurs when we are not creating from the pool of creative potential by inputting our full awareness into the ordering process. When this happens, we are, most often generating from the five senses bestowed on our human form. This form of design is imbalanced as it reverses the creation process. Creation is the gateway that transitions chaos *into* order by way of using the divine, or God mind. When we create from our human awareness, we transition order back into chaos. Derived disorder, on the earth plane, leads to confusion and ultimately imbalance.

In our nation/community building work we use the Kuumbic charge to reverse the harmful forms of creation back into their divine intentions by way of willful creation. This conscious creation is done by ascribing the completeness of our higher awareness into the ordering process, to create a scheme of cosmic order in the planet and heavens.

THE 14 KEYS

IMANI (FAITH)

"To believe with all our heart in our people, our parents, our teachers, our leaders and the righteousness and victory of our struggle."

Respectfully, I propose that now is the time to proceed beyond belief, acknowledging we have to come into an era of knowing. This begins with us discerning who our people, parents, teachers, and leaders are. Faith is the dive into the abyss of the unseen world, but only because the dive is necessary. It is our acuity to tap beyond what we passively accept with a proactive commitment of our entire beings. Faith is the only reality we accept, while concurrently concocting it.

Belief easily survives without challenge. When our beliefs are challenged we can sink into the unseen emotional confirmations that our feelings supply us with or we can use that as an opportunity to become seekers. In modern times, especially in light of the recently passing piscean age, belief has ruled out over truth in the hearts of many. Truth is gifted to the courageous explorer who is unafraid to dig beneath the surface of testimony.

Faith has to move beyond our intellectual or emotional acceptance. Our Imani (faith) is our stance between what we know and what we foresee. Commitment of faith has to be so radical that we are willing to sacrifice our entire allotment of life for what it is we invest our faith in. In light of the foregoing statement, if we were intelligently to distinguish faith from mere belief, the list of what we would be willing to die/live for may become very meager.

When we knowingly abandon the foundations of what we stand on, faith is what enmeshes us while in a mid air leap from one foundation to the next. It is the commitment of a strike that requires our four limbs and full body mass, in order to conquer an obstacle by choosing to commit our entire life to our knowing.

What we elect to put our faith in can not just be a result of our submission to reason or because of the evangelicalism of someone else's testimony. Our faith is revealed in our actions, not in our professed acceptance. Untested faith becomes belief when handed down without a true rite of passage experience and it must be applied and tested. Faith is the bridge that we are willing to traverse. Belief is the bridge that we send others down but, are afraid that it may not hold our own weight. Our bridges of faith, incontestably, are worth our trust.

Faith is a **knowing** in that which is not seen. When we begin to consider the work needed in community building, at this stage in the human time line, much of what we envision will exist only in mental arrangement. If community builders were to rely on facts or the supporting evidence of our material reality we would "see" that our situation is habitually turning against our favor. Faith goes beyond the temporal situating of facts. Facts can be manipulated. Facts can vacillate. Facts can even be revealed as the public opinion of the majority and are not, necessarily, true. Truth lies under that which is temporal as an eternal dynamic.

Faith requires us to plug back into our first eye reality whilst sharing a joint vision that may only exist in the realm inhabited by our collective higher selves. In the realm where truth lives, what we are and what we experience is an eternal stage of energetic interplay. What forms itself in the material realm, only forms itself for transitory reasons. These temporary formations are what we consider to be fact and palpable substantiation. That which can be audited by our sensual and intellectual capacities will always belong within the realm of material. The material realm is governed by the human brain. A devotion to humanism, is a devotion to lower discipline reasoning. Faith calls us to reason with our divine mind. The celestial mind is the cocreator of our lives orchestration and event sequencing. With this mind we can even see our end, as it highlights our lines of self-determination.

Those who choose to tune into the pulse of the human condition will notice the impermanence of all creation. This fading away of that which has manifested lead some to look for the essential forces that are always left after that evaporation.

Kobayashi Issa stated, "The world of dew — A world of dew it is indeed, And yet, and yet . . .".

In this amazing poem the Japanese poet, Kobayashi Issa, is speaking of the transitory nature of the world and the "yet" he speaks of is our driving nature to look underneath the impermanence and uncover that which remains. The "yet" is the call to examine life and move beyond the facts and beliefs, that fade, in order to discover the underlying meaning in, even, the temporary appearance of the elements that make up the world.

Faith does not demand an immovable spiritual devotion to one doctrine. Spiritual doctrines should be as alive and dynamic as the spiritual intelligences that conceive them. Faith drives us to deem how truth expands by actively engaging our beliefs.

To establish functional communities we have to go beyond group pride and presumed group superiority. There must be a distributed vision that is equal in value to the dearness of life. If the vision is not worth living or dying for, it will fade as all impermanent things do. Our human condition is a temporary one. The sojourn of our reflected soul is eternal so, our faith must make its contracts at the soul level and the human form will naturally follow suite. Once this occurs, the community will pulse with the ebb and flow of truth's movement and in every moment faith can be tested, applied, and put into action.

True faith cannot be generated but rather is received, as knowledge is. Individuals are drawn into a faith as male and female are attracted into a coupling. Faith extends beyond intellectual and sensory processing. In our Imani/faith we know we are the creator that claims what will be. When we put faith in the members of our communities, they become the collective higher realm's vision. For faith to work in a group, there must be a liberal amount of high vibrational bonding and spiritual communing among members. Faith grows in ourselves, and communities, as we proceed to carry out the orders of our soul mission. The group, itself, also has a "soul" mission. At times we will think our talents are insufficient to carry out the work of the mission but, if we have faith that we are purposely called and planted inside our given communities then that grasping will show us the divine vision of ourselves, and each other as conquerors. Jointly we overcome doubt, fear, obstacles, ego, and inadequacy. Investments in faith equip us for the task.

"I am the greatest, I said that even before I knew I was." - Muhammad Ali

CHIEF YUYA

LINKING THE CONCEPTS

CHIEF YUYA

THE 14 KEYS

In this section we are going to address the symbiosis between the internal concepts of Maat and the external ones of the Nguzo Saba. The internal theorems represent the unseen stimulus that produce the external state. The inner principles can be seen as contractile and feminine while the externals ones, expansive and masculine.

KEY CORRESPONDENCE

INTERNAL	EXTERNAL
Harmony	Umoja
Truth	Kujichagulia
Justice	Ujaama
Reciprocity	Ujima
Righteousness	Nia
Order	Kuumba
Balance	Imani

A contractile principle is one that blankets the seeker in its value and nurtures interior development. The external idea is the means by which that inner principle is carried out and manifested. Maat is a matriarchal archetype who sustains the unseen, or underlying, strength of a well-situated community and nation. It is no accident that Maat is personified as a wombmyn. The Nguzo Saba provides a set of working pursuits that methodize the members of a community to vocationally advance the decorum and success of the group.

The internal principles can, and should, be applied externally and the external principles applied internally. There are negative (contractible) and positive (expansive) polarities which can house any of the 14 keys. Polarities are not absolute. There is positive within negativity, and vice versa. This allows for an incorporating of combined keys, brilliantly at a minimum of 196 conceptions.

CHIEF YUYA

UMOJA-HARMONY

Harmony is necessary for the achieving of true unity. When we learn to develop and cherish the resonance of our own personal frequencies we can better accompany the work of others without violating the natural boundaries of our comrades. Knowing your note is vital to knowing who to harmonize with, and how.

Once this harmonic convergence is achieved the individuals involved create a new assemblage that appears to be one compulsion working in perfect unison with its chosen purpose. There is an insinuated difference among a group of individuals united in purpose versus a group of individuals united by motivating factors. A lynch mob can stir in unison however, the nucleic charge of each participant may not be creating a natural harmonic tone for the entire group. Participants may inherit displeasing karma or as it is said, "being in the wrong place at the wrong time" realism.

A synchronous harmony must be the objective for any true unification pursuit. It is not enough to just feel united. If harmony is not present, the participants will not receive the healing, fortune, or good karma that mission may offer. Harmony is the initiator of individuals into a mission which through work, time, and commitment will **lead** to true unity.

An individual whose internal vibration is not melodious and contains a harmonic discordancy among spirit, soul, mind, and body is a gathering of confused and broken spirits. Therefore a person with this level of inner ailment, reflects and projects that same inner melee throughout whatever it is they choose to create. There is also the distinct possibility that this condition can spread among those with whom this being has partnered with. Internal disharmony, surely leads to external disharmony. There can be no true unity without true harmony. True harmony begins within the single individual, and their characteristic note.

Umoja without harmony is not unity of the soul but, the corralling of the damaged. Albeit it is still a form of unity but without the other principles, the disharmonious frequencies and notes of the individual create an imbalanced family, community, and nation.

A lack of concordant harmony causes vibratory clashes and waves reflecting the same.

Our thoughts, emotions, and spirits must work in concert with the soul.

CHIEF YUYA

TRUTH - KUJICHAGULIA

Truth is a living cognition with an artful nature. Truth sits at the foundations of the universal wisdom shared among world cultures. The identical vein that runs through various religions and spiritual practices is the manifestation of the self determining nature of truth. Planet-wide truths are branches from the same root. Diversification is its means of survival. By being self defining, self determining, self naming, and self owning truth finds new branches of growth.

Truth is the sincere form of all forces so, when those forces create a character which defines its own avatar, truth distributes. This core essential substance, we call truth, is the will of all phenomena. It has no inclination of morality so it cannot be regulated to good or bad. Truth is not judged by its manifestations but, by its relevancy to the quality of the observers life.

Those who are purposed to extend their rationing of the truth substance beyond themselves carry the burden of the "teacher" avatar. A teacher differs from an educator. A teacher projects truths outwards, while an educator draws the truth out of an individual. In either case both, teacher and educator, are often despised for their clear sense of self and their determining of boundaries and responsibility.

Many do not want the responsibility of a free mind that functions from a truth imperative, nor do they want the control accountability that comes along with self-determination. Manifesting purpose in the context of a local or global community may require the individual to take on an unpopular role because the spirit of Kujichagulia that resides in the communal body mandates it. If that role has no previous plot for victory or it is a new adaptive position that the spirit of the community has created as a means of survival, it may require one to exist in relative social alienation inside of the communal body. This is when the faith of Kujichagulia is tested.

Rebelling against an established order is not requisitely an act of self-definition or self reclamation. The rebellion must be rooted in truth. If a rebellion is rooted in authenticity then it will adapt and change as cogency grows by observation, experience, and research.

THE 14 KEYS

There is one truth with many avatars. The responsibility of those avatars are to model self determination so the apexes of truth can be expanded.

CHIEF YUYA

RECIPROCITY – UJAAMA

Reciprocal economics are the circulation of energy and power. This circulatory system of a community is the active law of giving and receiving needed to encourage affluence and prosperity among community members. Here we see the magic and consciousness of our archetypes of wealth and love at work.

Our openness to give to others is no different from our openness to receive from others. Internal reciprocity is the natural flow of power and love, through our inner occupancy. The law of Karma is most active in this sphere of inner and external cause and effect. We engage life through reciprocity and the act of governing our life force, collectively.

Conscious choices maximize the vehicle of reciprocity and Ujaama in our lives. A compulsory biological function as simple as breathing duplicates a life-perpetual form of reciprocity. It has been well noted that breathing can be more than a mere auto-survival mechanism. Breathing is an actual art that can be studied, enhanced, and carried out as a tool for healing, such as with pranayama. Reciprocal cooperative economics is no different. We can negligently allow ourselves to become absorbed into a cartel of commercial trade or we can make a deliberate decision as to who we will share a system of full-bodied reciprocity with. Most often the economic matrix that we unconsciously participate in are not ones which benefit us but, rather the architects of those matrix.

Unconscious economics, or aloof causes, create effects that we normally do not want in our lives. Reciprocity is a form of economism, which is a form of love. The dangers of exchanging capital unconsciously can be equated to the dangers of mating inattentively. Ujaama/reciprocity/love are different terms that signify building or joint production. That product may be unity, group pride, group survival, self reproduction, or even escalated innerstanding.

The point of deliberation should be deciding if your internal choices create a burden on the life and existence of your community. We can introduce foreign poisons into our societal pool by exchanging our fiscal energy, brainlessly.

EVENHANDEDNESS-UJIMAA

Responsibility is the anchoring concept when these two ideas connect. A true community builder takes responsibility for their station, even if they are not to blame for their condition. Community builders need no one else to see their point of view.

The accountability that we can feel for each other, primarily comes without intellectual justification because it is primal. Consider the instinctive sense of protection that a parent has for their offspring. This level of care cannot be installed via intellectual assent.

Collective even-handedness instills a person's sense of belonging. Early on children are motivated by reward or punishment, within public environments. The accepted longing for reward or fear of penalty causes the child to look for validation from the public institutions. This, in and of itself, is not wrong if that institution is created and controlled by the adoring community the child sprang from. The way children are treated by a group, whether it be fair or unfair, is the indelible mark that stays within the psyche of a child even through their adult years. Children tend to look for conformance across the board when it comes to reward or punishment and expect the same level of treatment, typically. When this does not happen, they are quick to feel like disaffected outcast.

Justice, or even handedness, requires us to look for the suitable thing to do in the appropriate moment. In this way it is very similar to the law of righteousness. However, as justice moves to collective work and responsibility it uses the paradigms of *who* the community needs right now to pronounce what the rewards and punishments should be and which actions are acceptable. The "who" is created via reward and punishment.

Even handedness is the administration of the law. The edict that is enacted among a social group becomes the spiritual disposition of that faction. Law is incarnate spirit. This means group perception and conception of justice, even on an individual level, becomes the living spirit of that group because of its potential to define a group. Even handedness also provisions the jurisdictions of a group. So if that becomes the spirit of the group, the drive of collective work and responsibility produces the same exact character of the spirit of law that is passed forward from the administration of the law of the group collective. Ujimaa creates intergenerational stability, accountability, and a sense of inclusive value among individuals.

THE 14 KEYS
RIGHTEOUSNESS - NIA

A righteous purpose is a call within a community that anchors a person to their character. The dilemmas and enigmas of those communities are solved by individuals with the courage to engage their honorable Nia with the faith and conviction of valiant community warriors. A community breeds and sustains its own spirit. The communal spirit begins to engage the unseen parallel of the ancestral elements of the community and conveys the needs of the group members. As individuals are brought back through the ancestral pool into the world of the "living", they come with the solutions the community needs. In righteous purpose there is a relevant pretext for each character that community calls for and manufactures.

Regardless of how inconsequential a person may think their life purpose to be, by mere occurrence it verifies its vital importance. A soulless individual would lack the creative will and essence that the higher intelligence is comprised of. It is this very essence that holds the question, or purpose of the human manifestation of the "01" (Supreme Being). One without the living breath known as "soul" would be not of "God-Kin" and therefore purposeless. The existence of a purpose denotes the presence of the All Mighty.

Though difficult, outside the framework of a group or communal structure one can still unsheathe what their purpose is. However, an individual more easily finds the righteous relevancy of their purpose within the context of a group.

Righteousness is doing what is needed, right now.

Our purposes, even those that seem more theoretical, are still a part of a requisitioned solution. That solution is requested by the amalgamation of soul energy known as "Akasha" or "God".

Internal righteousness is the relevancy of the total person. All who receive the breath of life are born full of light or righteousness. This imparts a recognizing of identity and station in the cosmos. Without birth divination and true Eldership, as time passes and a deeper level of socialization occurs by authority figures, who have typically obscured their light, one loses sight of their status and longs for purpose. When this purpose is unveiled, their righteous-ness once again now has a vehicle of expression. Righteousness makes purpose crystal-clear and should be quested before first.

THE 14 KEYS
ORDER - KUUMBA

As we change the informational content of our intrinsic mind-sphere, we serially modify the information content of our outer-sphere. We create by what we have already positioned mentally. If we are unconsciously moving through life with no sense of balanced energy distribution, then our world reflects the same level of aimless hysteria.

Intention is internal. Intention is the child of will and will is a child of the soul. Intention, will, and order are cognitive attributes that operate inside our consciousness. We develop our working catalog of inventive matter internally. There are billions of thoughts that pass through our psyche throughout the course of our lives. The inner catalog we create are the calculations, inspirations, and ruminations that we surmise as requisite for the life we author. Our intention shapes and molds energy through transforming processes of thought to production.

Our attention sees its impact on the external providing vitality and life. There are times that our psyche orchestrates experiences where we are forced to give attention to certain events, sensations, or compulsions in our lives. This occurs because the visceral self is sending a message to our active consciousness. What we lend our attention to, we reanimate. There are times in our lives when we neglect certain components of our inner dominion, creating an imbalance. That imbalance leads to confusion. When the created is unaware, via neglect, of the intentions of the creator it begins to question its place in the scheme of formation. The created then will seek to take the place of the creator. The neglect that we serve upon our created becomes a neglect that the created serves upon us. At times, it becomes very difficult to master our spiritual kingdoms due to this neglect. If we spend most our lives ignoring the spiritual members that exist around us, the strength of the natural bond weakens.

Conscious formation requires conscious systematizing. Our conscious ordering has to be self determined. When we define ourselves, we balance ourselves. There are many things that we can be, and become, in a moment. Despite our high potential for elasticity, we must create relative avatars and descriptions of ourselves to fulfill the divine purpose that the originating Creator compelled.

Kuumbic ordering charges us to order better causes for ourselves so that we may fruitfully create a more purposeful reality.

THE 14 KEYS
BALANCE-IMANI

There is a sacred connectivity that merges all forces in creation. These forces are part of an organism that is called, the "Universe". The prefix "uni" distinguishes a oneness. The perceived oneness of all things are held in balance by the raw materials of the cosmic mind.

Reverence for the vital faculties that govern proportion throughout nature begins the deputation of faith. Unseen sources and drives have made an appearance in the world of matter. Regardless of what is beheld in the corporeal, and the complexity of that embodiment, the manifestation is an echoed image of a truer unseen order. We can compare this with the relationship between our thoughts and our words. Often what we think does not convey precisely through our verbiage. However, it doesn't take away from the palpability that our words are a product of our thoughts. Each one needs the other. Thoughts need a vehicle of exhibition so they can properly be expelled from our mental womb. Words need the supporting composition and meanings that the evaluations behind them provide. These two phenomena have to be held in conscience balance to sustain the unseen and seen authenticity. Hence, the faith that we have and what is produced from the surety of our thought becomes stronger.

Balance is a commitment, because beyond the speculation of the veracity of what is unseen or the genuineness of what is *seeing*, there comes a middle line trust. This middle line trust becomes the equaling point between the realms of "heaven" and the province of "hell". That balancing point uses intellectualism, but also uses the sense of purpose that all individuals host in the seat of their hearts. This is the equalizing point. It is no coincidence that the heart chakra is the middle point among the three major chakras beneath it and the three major chakras above it. It is a convergent point where forces can be made equal.

Faith is often considered to be something that requires a wholehearted commitment. The heart even provides a balancing point for our emotions of connectedness and disconnectedness. The ideas and emotions of love and hate both emanate from the heart.

CHIEF YUYA

So we find the decision that is made between the two occurs within that middle line trust. These are the deliberations that occur in the unseen that then govern faithful actions. Our methods of balancing project to actions of faith that require the entire physical, emotional, intellectual, and spiritual body.

THE 14 KEYS

CHIEF YUYA

CONCLUSION

CHIEF YUYA

THE 14 KEYS

In this work I have stressed the importance of the adaptive nature of *all* the 14 keys for inner transformation and group creation. These keys are still morphing OUR living traditions. All forces that contain the essence of life have the potential to change. Often, we see truth as a static and disassociated entity. We, who engage the deep thought of Ancestral wisdom, become architects of the advancing traditions.

The total formula involves the alchemical character development as provide by the principles of Maat and the social alignment of the Nguzo Saba. Without a coherent moralistic will for cohesion, unity becomes unprincipled havoc. Organizing into functional groups for a healthy purpose, requires order that is a working fusion of the laws of transformation and the gems of the principles of harvesting.

I purposely have not expounded, extensively, on the sources of the interpretations of Maat or the history Dr. Maulana Karenga. I intend the reader to take personal ownership of the principles they are, willfully, integrating into their life. Cosmic principles are the wealth of all inhabitants of the plan-et. They can be channeled through those who are in step with the divine rhythm and ego-less enough to receive. Dr. Karenga and the authors of the Pert Em HRU were just this. All authors of holy (sun) books of divine formulas are but conduits being ceremonially possessed by high functioning spiritual archetypes. **We all have this potential.**

We are still engaged in our ongoing creative process as creator and created, producing a more beautiful creation via vertical inner refinement.

Applying this manuscript is a humble step we can all take towards effective awakening. Without a collectively agreed on edict, there is no community. We can implant a community of the dysfunctional or we can embrace the internal counsel of Maat in order to work the authentic magic, we are seeking and *commonly professing.* As the Nguzo Saba tells us, this work is an ongoing struggle and these are principles that we must strive to manifest. There is no easy road to actualization or communal self determination but, with the right tools we can carve the right paths for ourselves and loved ones.

Keep striving,

Chief YUYA

CHIEF YUYA

For an online course that shows you how you can apply the 14 keys in your life please go to :

Saduluhouse.com/courses/the-14-keys

There you will find videos, hands-on exercises, and audio that help you on your journey of innerstanding and applying the 14 keys in your life!

SaduluHouse.com/Store

ABOUT THE AUTHOR

H. Yuya T. Assaan-ANU is the founder of "ANU Nation", head of "ANU Life Global Ministries", and an enstooled chief in Nigeria and Ghana, West Africa. As an ordained minister, initiated high priest, and social educator he has taught the greater public, internationally, for over 25 years. Chief operates an NGO in Central region of Ghana which serves as a bridge of cultural exchange and provides computer technology to local villages throughout West Africa. A renown spiritual guide, Chief has taught many through the Sadulu House spiritual center and the Enlightenment and Transformation broadcast platform. Chief Yuya has a demonstrated mastery of Orisha/Ifa tradition, community building, youth empowerment, self-actualization, family creation, African philosophy, and economic warfare.

Books:

Chief Yuya is also the author of the following titles:
"Shrine and Altar"
"Grasping the Root of Divine Power"
"Solutions for Dysfunctional Family Relationships"

For Books, Videos, and Products go to:

AlphaOmegaStore.com

Classes:

Yuya teaches classes on spiritual growth, personal development, and indigenous ancient spirituality. Classes bring a person through the beginner to advanced level of spirit and soul work in a very hands on practical manner.

To enroll in a class you can go to SaduluHouse.com.

Connect with Chief Yuya Online:
Instagram : Instagram.com/ChiefYuya
Twitter: Twitter.com/ChiefYuya
Facebook: Facebook.com/ChiefYuya
ANU Publishing: ANU-Bookstore.com
ANU Nation: ANUNation.org
Broadcast: EnlightenmentandTransformation.com

www.ingramcontent.com/pod-product-compliance
Lightning Source LLC
LaVergne TN
LVHW051605080426
835510LV00020B/3148

* 9 7 8 0 9 9 8 0 9 6 6 0 5 *